GETTING STARTED WITH ARIZONA PROBATE

GETTING STARTED WITH ARIZONA PROBATE

Scott David Stewart, Esq.

Brian G. Winter, Esq.

An Imprint of Stewart Law Group

www.ArizonaLawGroup.com

SDS Legal Marketing LLC USA, Publisher
777 E Thomas Rd Ste 150, Phoenix AZ 85014
sdslegalmarketing.com

FIRST EDITION
ISBN 978-1-7323041-2-3

For information please write the publisher:

SDS Legal Marketing LLC
777 E Thomas Rd Ste 150
Phoenix AZ 85014

Legal Disclaimer

The general information in this book is not, nor is it intended to be, specific legal advice. You should consult an attorney for specific legal advice regarding your individual situation and circumstances.

This book is provided as a general reference work and is for informational purposes only. You are advised to check for changes to current law and to consult with a qualified attorney on any legal issue. The receipt of or use of this book does not create an attorney-client relationship with Stewart Law Group, its principals, or any of its attorneys.

Because this book was prepared for general readership without investigation into the facts of each particular case, it is not legal advice. Neither Stewart Law Group nor any of its attorneys has an attorney-client relationship with you. The thoughts and commentary about the law contained in this book are provided merely as a public service and do not constitute solicitation or legal advice.

While we endeavored to provide accurate information in this book, we cannot guarantee that the material provided herein is accurate, adequate, or complete. This general legal information is provided on an 'as is' basis. We make no warranties and disclaim liability for damages resulting from its use. Legal advice must be tailored to the specific circumstances of each case and laws are constantly changing. Therefore, nothing provided in this book should be used as a substitute for the advice of competent legal counsel.

The material in this book may be considered advertising under applicable rules.

Chapter

Acknowledgements

My thanks to all the attorneys with Stewart Law Group for their professionalism and dedication to assisting clients and improving the legal profession. To Laura Valade, J.D., for her diligent research and editing. And to my family for keeping me motivated and for reminding me of life's many blessings.

A Personal Message...

When a client asks me about Arizona probate, I know something serious has happened. The passing of a parent, child, or loved one is difficult, whether family remains close or has drifted apart over the years.

First of all, allow yourself time to grieve. These can be intensely emotional situations with substantial financial and legal concerns. Sorting out the details of another's life means remembering what was forgotten and being surprised by things previously unknown.

Decisions are much tougher when loved ones are at the heart of the matter. Begin moving forward with legal guidance from an experienced probate attorney. We ease the stress of these proceedings by doing our jobs very well. Some lawyers won't handle contested cases or appeals. We do. You can count on us to litigate your case and file an appeal when necessary.

There is a light at the end of the tunnel. You will get through this.

Scott David Stewart

1

Everyone Needs a Probate Introduction

Most people experience Arizona probate proceedings with the passing of a loved one. Even if you have been through probate administration following the death of a parent, spouse, sibling, child, or more distant family member, your current role may be quite different. When thrust into this legal situation, there is much to process. As you will see, probate law covers more than decedents' estates.

Because estate planning and probate are inextricably linked, email *bookorders@ArizonaLawGroup.com* to request our companion eBook – **Getting Started with Arizona Estate Planning**.

Where to Start?

First, know your rights and responsibilities. Hire a competent attorney, you need a trusted professional to consult as proceedings unfold. There is always the possibility of probate litigation. Determine the pros and cons and risk of liability for actions taken, if any. For instance, an heir could object to the Personal Representative's proposed distribution, alleging unfairness and self-dealing. Similarly, because a Trustee serves in a fiduciary capacity, a breach of that duty could expose the Trustee to liability.

Second, know the steps to be taken in your case. This will depend upon the petition filed with the Probate Clerk of the Superior Court. Consider some examples:

- **Testate Succession:** You were nominated Personal Representative (Executor) in the deceased's Last Will and Testament.
- **Will Validity:** You are an heir who believes the Testator lacked capacity to execute a Will or someone exerted undue influence over the Testator and, therefore, challenge its validity.

- **Intestate Succession:** The decedent did not have a Last Will and Testament when he or she died and you need to be appointed Personal Representative of the intestate estate.
- **Trust Administration:** As Trustee, you request clarification and instructions from the court on how to proceed with trust administration.
- **Beneficiary Rights:** You are one of several beneficiaries contesting the terms of a Trust.
- **Minor Guardianship:** You were appointed the testamentary Guardian in the Last Will and Testament and want to formalize the decedent's wishes and be formally appointed the legal Guardian of the minor child.
- **Adult Guardianship:** You petitioned the court to be appointed the Guardian of an incapacitated or incapable adult so that you can legally make decisions concerning the person's health and welfare.
- **Conservatorship:** You petitioned the court to be appointed the Conservator of an incapacitated or incapable adult so that you can legally make decisions concerning the person's estate and financial affairs.

All of those matters require thoughtful consideration of the issues presented. They also represent the types of legal matters our probate attorneys routinely handle. Although litigation can happen even between family members, mediation and settlement conferences are available to help resolve disputes.

Many legal matters fall within the jurisdiction of the probate court, but we have limited these pages to Wills and intestate succession, Guardianships and Conservatorships, and probate litigation generally. Don't be discouraged if your situation does not fall neatly into one of those categories or involves some non-probate transfer. Call us. Talk to a caring professional who can help.

2

Probate and Decedents Estates from the Beginning

When a person passes on, property owned in life becomes property of the "decedent's estate." This could include real estate, intellectual property, stocks and bonds, vehicles, jewelry, antiques, art collections, books, business interests, personal items, and a lifetime's worth of memorabilia. The decedent's estate will eventually be distributed to those entitled to it by law. Property is conveyed and assets are transferred to heirs, devisees, and trust beneficiaries.

The individual who serves as Personal Representative (Executor) steps in and takes control. There are many loose ends to tie up, from payment of utilities and rent or mortgages to marshalling financial accounts. The only way to really know how to move forward is to get involved and seek legal guidance as you go.

What About Creditors?

The decedent's creditors will be paid from the estate before a final distribution is made. Debts include home mortgages, credit card statements, medical expenses, funeral and burial expenses, and taxes, to name a few. Some creditor claims may be paid in full, other claims may be avoided, while others may be reduced or forgiven. Much can be accomplished by the Personal Representative through diligence and settlement.

What Is Probate?

The term "probate" means two things. First, probate is the legal process of proving validity of the Last Will and Testament. Second, probate is the judicial process of overseeing administration of the decedent's estate.

If the decedent had a Will, then the case proceeds under testate succession law. Without a valid Will, the case proceeds under intestate succession law.

An interested party may challenge validity of the Will, but there must be legal grounds. By way of example only, a pretermitted or disinherited heir alleges the decedent lacked testamentary capacity having been diagnosed with advanced dementia three months before executing the purported Will. A Will contest is litigation so consult an attorney. Dissatisfaction with some minor aspect of administration or dislike for the person nominated as the Personal Representative is unlikely to be successful. It takes more.

Superior Court Has Probate Jurisdiction

Where do you file your probate case? The Arizona Constitution grants the Superior Court original jurisdiction over all matters of probate — trusts, estates, and protective proceedings. Ariz. Const. art. 6, § 14. In those court proceedings, the *Arizona Rules of Probate Procedure* will apply.

As for substantive law, there is Title 14 of the Arizona Revised Statutes and an extensive body of case law. Federal law may also apply to the case, as with estate and gift taxes.

3

Small Estates and Summary Probate

Not every decedent's estate warrants lengthy probate proceedings. Yes, small estates and summary proceedings fall within the probate court's jurisdiction.

Collecting Property from a Small Estate

Arizona probate law allows for the use of three types of affidavits when no Personal Representative is appointed. Certain family members or a sole heir can utilize the affidavit process. Other conditions must be met, too, so it's not for everyone. Still, the affidavit process can substantially reduce the cost of estate administration and really speed things up. Take a look at the three affidavits.

Affidavit for Collection of Personal Property

The first affidavit is used to collect personal property owned by the decedent up to a value of $75,000. ARS § 14-3971(B).

Affidavit for Transfer of Title to Real Property

The second affidavit is used to transfer real property with an assessed value, less liens and encumbrances, of up to $100,000. ARS § 14-3971(E).

Affidavit for Collection of Wages

The third affidavit lets the surviving spouse collect up to $5,000 in wages owed the decedent. Is more than $5,000 owed? Use regular probate proceedings to collect any amount of wages in excess of $5,000. ARS § 14-3971(A).

For many families, the decedent's entire estate can be summarily collected and distributed to those entitled to it by law.

Using Summary Probate

When a Personal Representative is appointed to administer a small estate, summary probate proceedings may be an alternative. Without having to notify creditors, the Personal Representative may immediately disburse and distribute the estate to those entitled to it if, and only if, the value of the entire estate, less liens and encumbrances, does not exceed the:

> "[A]llowance in lieu of homestead, exempt property, family allowance, costs and expenses of administration, reasonable funeral expenses, and reasonable and necessary medical and hospital expenses of the last illness of the decedent..."
>
> ARS § 14-3974.

How does someone get appointed Personal Representative? That's in the next lesson.

4

Initiating Informal Probate of Decedent's Estate

There are several phases to the probate process. You can download informal probate instructions and forms directly from the Superior Court's website at *http://superiorcourt.maricopa.gov*. Just so you know, there are no instructions or forms available for complex cases requiring Formal Probate and substantial judicial oversight.

Now then, let's start with an overview of how the typical informal probate case proceeds. Be mindful, any case can take on legal twists and turns.

I. Appointment of Personal Representative

The individual who is appointed Personal Representative by the court is responsible for the administration of the decedent's estate. These are fiduciary duties and should be taken seriously.

Who may be appointed Personal Representative when the decedent died intestate? If there was no Will, then only someone legally connected to the decedent may seek appointment and initiate informal probate proceedings.

To be appointed Personal Representative, the petitioner must be related to the deceased person (the surviving spouse, adult child, parent, or sibling) or have some legal interest in decedent's property. (If 45 days after the death no petition is filed, then a creditor may apply.) Having a legal background or accounting degree is not a requirement for this appointment.

Other family members often waive their right to appointment and may waive the bond requirement for the petitioner, too. Additionally, the court may limit the petitioner's authority by including restrictions in the Letters of Personal Representative.

Did decedent have a Will? Assuming the testator nominated someone to serve as the Personal Representative and that person accepts the nomination, then he or she applies to the probate court for Letters Testamentary. One way or another, someone will be appointed by the court to administer the decedent's estate. In some cases, that may be a court-appointed licensed fiduciary. Along with the appointment Letters, the court issues a Statement of Informal Probate with acknowledgement and information to heirs and devisees.

When to open Informal Probate? The need to access funds from the decedent's bank account is one reason to act swiftly. However, rarely are family members ready to proceed with probate immediately after the death of their loved one. Some may hesitate to act or respond, particularly when the death was unexpected. While trying to come to terms with a loved one's passing, consider opening a dialogue with a caring probate attorney. Having legal counsel ready to answer questions can be helpful at this time to allay fears and ease the transition into probate.

Be mindful of the window for filing informal probate: No sooner than 120 hours after the time of death and, with few exceptions, no later than two years after the time of death. ARS § 14-3108. Has it been over two years? Talk to your attorney about filing a petition to initiate Formal Probate proceedings.

2. Admission of the Last Will and Testament to Probate

Informal Probate of the Will includes filing the Will with the court for authentication. Validity of the Will must be determined. If the Will is valid on its face, meaning it satisfies all legal requirements or is self-proving, then the case moves forward to the next phase.

Is the Will defective? Additional evidence may be needed to validate the Will. The judge will either admit the Will or reject the instrument and proceed under the laws of intestate succession. Your attorney should prepare you for potential problems or defects in the Will early in the representation.

3. Court Approved Training

Before being appointed Personal Representative, you must complete the court-approved training module for non-licensed fiduciaries. File the Certificate of Completion with the court. (The same requirement holds for Guardians and Conservators.)

You will be very glad you went through this training! Not only will the training modules provide guidance, but they will help you avoid the common mistakes and misunderstandings that lead to objections from heirs, devisees, or creditors.

What Are the Personal Representative's Duties?

- To marshal estate assets while observing the standard of care required by law.
- To exercise all duties fairly and impartially as a fiduciary.
- To notify interested persons of the appointment and admission of the Will to probate.
- To mail copies of the court's Order to Personal Representative to heirs, devisees, and those who filed demand for notice.
- To publish Notice to Creditors in a newspaper of general circulation for three consecutive weeks and file with the court the Affidavit of Publication after the publication is complete. The Notice includes the decedent's name, probate case number and court, personal representative and probate attorney, contact information, the deadline for filing claims and how those claims must be submitted.
- To find, identify, take possession of, and protect all estate assets.
- To prepare an Inventory and Appraisement and keep detailed records.

- To apply statutory allowances under Arizona law.
- To pay debts, taxes, valid claims, and costs of administration (including attorney fees, appraisals, accountant fees, and other services).
- To keep records supporting the need for reimbursement and reasonable compensation if applicable.
- To distribute all assets from the estate to heirs, devisees, and beneficiaries.
- To provide a full written accounting.
- To wrap-up the estate and file a Closing Statement.

Understand that Personal Representatives are generally reimbursed from the estate for their out-of-pocket expenditures (for example, travel expenses, shipping costs, legal fees and filing fees).

Is the Personal Representative seeking *reasonable compensation* for services rendered? Arizona law does allow for this. ARS § 14-3719. Some estates are far more complex than others and being the point person can be quite challenging. Consider the Personal Representative who devoted 20 hours a week over a period of 14 months to administer the estate. Always keep good records of the time spent and receipts for any expenditures. Anyone with a legal interest in the decedent's estate may object to the Personal Representative's requested fees and request a judicial hearing.

4. Notice to Heirs, Devisees, Beneficiaries and Creditors

The Personal Representative's next task is notifying interested parties of the informal probate and appointment. Be sensitive to the possibility that some family members may be unaware of the death and take the news hard. Actual notice is sent in the mail to known heirs, devisees, and beneficiaries. (Even those who were told the details over the phone or in person should receive a written letter containing the details.)

An heir, devisee, or creditor of the estate may request supervised probate or Formal Probate. Supervised probate means the judge must approve each transaction the Personal Representative or executor intends to carry out. On the positive side, this assures administration of the estate is conducted properly with more judicial involvement in the case. On the negative side, Formal Probate will likely experience delays, increase costs of administration, and take longer to close. Although Formal Probate is necessary for some estates, most follow the path of unsupervised probate or informal probate with minimal judicial oversight.

An heir or devisee ordinarily has four months from receiving notice and information of informal probate to contest those proceedings and initiate Formal Probate. This is not an absolute time bar, however.

5. Statutory Allowances in Arizona Probate Law

What rights do surviving family members have? Allowances are a way of ensuring the spouse or decedent's children are not left destitute – assets are set aside just for them.

Three allowances are payable from the decedent's separate property and the decedent's share of the community property. Allowances have priority over all other claims to the estate but for expenses of administration. Take a look.

Homestead Allowance

The surviving spouse is entitled to a homestead allowance of $18,000. What if there is no surviving spouse? The homestead allowance is divided among the decedent's minor or dependent children. This allowance is chargeable against any benefit passing to the surviving spouse or child. For example, if the wife's Will leaves $18,000 to her husband, then the full allowance is used. ARS § 14-2402.

Family Allowance

During probate administration, the surviving spouse and decedent's minor children need support. The family allowance provides that maintenance and support directly from the estate. Payment can be made in a lump sum or in periodic installments. What if the estate is insolvent? The allowance may continue for up to a year. With no surviving spouse, the child's Guardian would receive the funds on behalf of the minor. ARS § 14-2404. (Guardianship proceedings are discussed later.)

Exempt Property Allowance

The third allowance for the surviving spouse or decedent's child if no surviving spouse is $7,000 in estate furniture, furnishings, automobiles, appliances, and personal effects. If the aggregate value of those exempt assets are less than $7,000, then the spouse or child is entitled to other estate assets until the allowance amount is met. ARS § 14-2403.

The next phase of informal probate is estate administration and accounting. We'll take those up in the next lesson.

5
Basic Estate Administration and Accounting

Estate administration largely depends upon the assets and debts comprising it. Was the decedent a real estate investor? Then a Deed of Distribution may be required to transfer property to new owners. Did the decedent own vehicles? Title transfers will be necessary. The Personal Representative's job description includes doing whatever it takes to legally transfer assets out of the estate and into the hands of the new owners. To do this right, be willing to obtain professional advice from an accountant, attorney, broker, and other professional.

Inventory and Accounting

The Personal Representative marshals the estate, takes inventory, puts values on assets, lists debts, and accounts for estate expenses. Accounting refers to everything going into the estate and everything coming out of it. Bookkeeping not your forte? Delegate those tasks to a competent individual.

Unless the court appoints a Public Fiduciary, there is no requirement that the Personal Representative have special knowledge of law or accounting. Instead, obtain legal counsel and seek advice from an accountant. Does the estate include fine art? An appraiser can authenticate and value each piece, often arranging for auction as well.

Testate Estate Administration

With a testate estate, the Will controls testamentary gifts to named devisees, legatees, charities and beneficiaries. Say, for example, an adult child is devised the decedent's primary residence. That devisee either accepts or disclaims interest in the property.

If the devise is accepted (and most are), then the Personal Representative consults with the attorney and clears whatever hurdles are associated with the property before transferring it to the devisee. (If disclaimed, then the property goes to the next person entitled to it in the Will.) This could involve using estate assets to pay off the mortgage, prorating property taxes to the day of transfer, making repairs, and so on. The executor's duties are tied to the Will's terms and the nature of the estate.

Intestate Estate Administration

With an intestate estate where the person died without a Will, the heirs at law in classes of blood relationships to the decedent inherit. Arizona statutory law controls distribution of the decedent's estate. In other words, the statute becomes the decedent's estate plan.

Here's an example. The spouses had been married 15 years, a first marriage for both. Following her husband's death, the wife inherits the entire intestate estate. That includes her husband's separate property and his share of their community property. (The wife already owns the other half of the community property.) ARS § 14-2102.

Change the facts just a bit and the outcome is substantially different. This was the wife's first marriage, but the husband had a child from a previous marriage. Now the wife only inherits one-half of her husband's separate property. The other half of the decedent's separate property and his share of the community property passes to his child from the prior marriage.

Any portion of the intestate estate not passing to a surviving spouse goes to the following heirs who survive the decedent in the following order:

1. To the decedent's descendants by representation.

2. If there is no surviving descendant, to the decedent's parents equally if both survive or to the surviving parent.

3. If there is no surviving descendant or parent, to the descendants of the decedent's parents or either of them by representation.

4. If there is no surviving descendant, parent or descendant of a parent, but the decedent is survived by one or more grandparents or descendants of grandparents, half of the estate passes to the decedent's paternal grandparents equally if both survive or to the surviving paternal grandparent or the descendants of the decedent's paternal grandparents or either of them if both are deceased with the descendants taking by representation. The other half passes to the decedent's maternal relatives in the same manner. If there is no surviving grandparent or descendant of a grandparent on either the paternal or the maternal side, the entire estate passes to the decedent's relatives on the other side in the same manner as the half.

ARS § 14-2103.

What if no one is qualified to claim the decedent's estate? Although this rarely occurs, the entire intestate estate passes to the State of Arizona. ARS § 14-2105.

Yes, intestate succession can be confusing. Protect your rights and avoid problems by keeping an open dialogue with your lawyer.

6
Guardianship of Children

Many people assume Guardianship is just for children and Conservatorship is for adults. But a Guardian may also be appointed for an incapacitated adult and a Conservator appointed for a minor child.

Think of Guardianship as caring for the person while Conservatorship involves managing the person's legal and financial matters. Still, there is an overlap. Every case is unique, but sometimes it makes sense for the same individual to serve as both Guardian and Conservator.

In Arizona, only the Superior Court sitting in probate has authority to appoint Guardians and Conservators and issue Letters of Appointment. These are serious matters. Do your homework and consult an attorney at every step.

Appointing a Guardian for the Minor Child

Probate proceedings to appoint a minor's guardian differ in some ways from those involving adult wards. For one, any appointment must be in the best interests of the child. ARS § 14-5206.

Who Can Be Appointed Guardian of a Minor?

Guardianship of a child is solely based on minority status – the child's age. Although there are additional conditions to be met, the following two appointments are possible.

1. Testamentary Appointment

The parent's Will nominated a Guardian who either accepts or declines appointment. ARS § 14-5202. Importantly, if the minor is 14 years of age or older, then he or she may object to the testamentary appointment. ARS § 14-5203.

2. Court Appointment

The probate judge can appoint a Guardian when parental custody rights have been terminated or legally suspended. ARS § 14-5204. This includes the unfortunate situation where a parent predeceases the child without nominating a Guardian in the Will. And not every testamentary nominee accepts appointment. If acceptance of testamentary appointment does not occur within the time allowed, then the court will appoint another interested person to take responsibility for the child.

Although the typical minor Guardianship terminates upon adulthood, some individuals will need Guardians as adults, too. If the child turns 18 and is incapacitated, then proceedings for appointment of a Guardian for this young adult should take place without a lapse in supervision and care.

In certain circumstances, a licensed private fiduciary may be appointed Guardian. Importantly, a Conservator is frequently appointed along with the Guardian of a minor. Sometimes the same adult serves as both Guardian and Conservator. Every case is unique, so talk to an experienced probate attorney about your specific situation.

Who Will Be the Child's Guardian?

If you were nominated in the deceased parent's Will and file a written acceptance, absent objection, the probate court will issue Letters of Guardianship. Although it's good practice, some Wills do not include Guardianship clauses.

What if you desire appointment, but were not nominated in the parent's Will? Petition the court for an Order of Guardianship. First, appointment must be in the child's best interests. Second, the child must have a significant relationship with you by blood, marriage, or friendship. ARS § 14-5101(14). The child may have a living parent (biological or adoptive) and still need a Guardian. In that situation, the parent may consent to appointment.

Do You Qualify for Appointment?

The following persons may seek appointment as Guardian or Conservator of a minor:

- Someone already appointed Guardian or Conservator by a court in the jurisdiction where the minor lives.
- The minor is age 14 or older, nominated the petitioner and, in the court's opinion, has the mental capacity to choose intelligently.

- The spouse of the minor.
- Someone nominated in the deceased parent's Will.
- The child's relative (but not the parent) if the child lived with him or her more than six months before filing the petition.
- A person caring for or paying benefits to the minor nominated the petitioner.
- A private fiduciary or public fiduciary licensed in Arizona. ARS § 14-5651.

What if you don't fit into one of those categories? Explain your connection with the minor and why your appointment is in the child's best interests. Any petitioner who is not related to the child by blood must provide fingerprints to the court to enable a criminal background check within five days of filing the petition. ARS § 14-5206.

Just so you know, court-approved training modules must be completed before the probate hearing.

Role of the Minor's Guardian

What exactly does the minor's Guardian do? Although there are legal limits, what the job entails will depend upon the needs of the child. A Guardian is not a parent, but in many ways that is the role you will serve. Allow as much independence and self-determination as possible given the child's age, developmental stage, education, special needs, health issues, and so on.

Every Guardian has a duty to be informed about each concern facing the child before consenting to a particular course of action. Only after full disclosure of the facts can the Guardian make intelligent decisions on behalf of the Ward.

As the child's Guardian, you will have the following responsibilities:

- Make certain the Ward's medical and mental health concerns are covered;
- Keep records and document every aspect of your decision-making;
- Apply for and ensure the Ward receives all government benefits and entitlements;
- Manage up to $10,000 of the Ward's money if a Conservator has not been appointed;
- Prepare and file an annual Guardianship Report with the Court;
- Notify the court immediately of any change to the Ward's address;
- File a Notice of Compensation if paid from the Ward's estate for services as Guardian;
- Track out-of-pocket expenses for reimbursement from the Ward's estate; and

- Hire the services of an attorney when necessary for the Ward.

Next, we'll look at Guardians for adult Wards. As you will see, not every disabled adult needs a Guardian. And not every Guardianship is permanent.

7

Appointing a Guardian for an Incapacitated Adult

The probate judge has authority to appoint a Guardian for an incapacitated adult.

What is meant by incapacitated? An incapacitated person is unable to make or communicate responsible decisions for himself or herself. More specifically, the person "is impaired by reason of mental illness, mental deficiency, mental disorder, physical illness or disability, chronic use of drugs, chronic intoxication or other cause..." ARS § 14-5101(3). The protected person might be an elderly man with dementia, for example, or young woman with a traumatic brain injury.

There is the possibility of limited guardianship where the Ward's right to vote is restored. After petition and hearing, the probate judge must determine by clear and convincing evidence that this adult retains sufficient understanding to exercise his or her right to vote.

The Guardian's responsibilities will differ depending upon the Ward's age, health, mental condition, and so on. Generally, the Guardian of an adult Ward is responsible for arranging housing, meals, clothing, personal care needs, healthcare, medical services, therapy, and social or group activities.

Because the Guardian has so many responsibilities and the adult Ward has rights to protect, the Guardian reports annually to the court. The ultimate question to be answered is "Does this Ward still need a Guardian?" If "No," then the Guardianship should be terminated.

Guardianship for six months or longer is considered "permanent." If the Guardianship is less than six months, then the appointment is "temporary." A temporary appointment could be followed by permanent appointment or no appointment.

Can the Guardian institutionalize an adult Ward? No. Some adults worry a Guardian might take away their freedoms, but Guardianship is not without limitation. Commitment to a mental health facility is not possible without a court order. (Note, under certain circumstances a temporary 72-hour hold is possible.) At the hearing, the Ward must be proven gravely disabled before the Court will order commitment.

What if Guardianship is no longer needed? There are many reasons why Guardianship should come to an end, such as death of an elderly Ward or complete recovery. The Guardian can ask the court to terminate Guardianship and discharge the Guardian. The Ward or an interested party (such as the Ward's spouse or adult child) may also petition the court to terminate the Guardianship.

Does the Guardian charge a fee for services? Sometimes. Certainly, the Guardian has substantial responsibilities, but that is not to say tapping into the Ward's bank account is proper. The Guardian is only entitled to be paid a reasonable fee and must get the probate judge's approval. ARS § 14-5314.

Arizona law tells us who may be appointed Guardian of either a minor or incapacitated adult. ARS § 14-5311. The Will may nominate a Guardian, but only the probate court can appoint someone to that role.

8
Understanding Conservatorship

The probate process of appointing a Conservator is known as a protective proceeding. ARS § 14-5401. The Conservator is a fiduciary. In managing the Ward's property, the fiduciary is in a position of utmost trust and confidence.

Upon appointment, the Conservator focuses on taking control of and protecting the protected person's assets. This means marshaling bank accounts, investments, real estate, and any other asset or ownership interest the Ward has. Everything the Conservator does is on behalf of the Ward and for that person's benefit. Because of the extensive financial responsibilities that come with the job, the Conservator posts bond sufficient to cover the value of the Conservatorship estate and its income for a year.

Duties of the Conservator

Let's take a look at the Conservator's role in the Ward's life. Whether appointment is temporary or permanent, the Conservator's duties include:

- Completing court-approved training;
- Posting surety bond;
- Obtaining a certified copy of Letters of Conservatorship and recording them where the Ward lives and owns property;
- Marshalling accounts with banks, credit unions, and financial institutions and retitling them in the Conservatorship;
- Retitling automobiles in the Conservatorship through MVD;
- Documenting all transactions;
- Documenting all assets;
- Obtaining a credit report on the Ward;
- Providing an opening Inventory and Appraisement of property for filing within 90 days of

appointment. The starting inventory should include all financial accounts, life insurance policies with a cash surrender value, motor vehicles, cash, collections, furniture and furnishings, and so on.

- Creating a budget and projecting how the economic needs of the Ward will be met with estate income, assets, and other resources (called Sustainability of Conservatorship);
- Notifying all creditors and service providers of the Conservatorship and any change of address;
- Keeping extensive records, including reimbursements for out-of-pocket expenses paid (such as court filing fees and attorney consultations);
- Filing the Annual Accounting;
- Filing Notice of Compensation for any fee the Conservator plans to charge; and
- Following applicable laws and complying with the court's orders. The probate judge can also impose restrictions on the Conservator's authority.

So long as no harm will result, the Conservator should listen to and follow the Ward's preferences. Doing what is in the best interests of the protected person is always number one. Before substituting judgment for that of the Ward's, discuss the issue with him or her. With some incapacitated individuals, however, that may not be feasible.

Mishandling the Estate

The surety bond protects the Ward in the event there is a loss to the estate as a result of the Conservator's mishandling or malfeasance. A fiduciary should always avoid conflicts of interest, such as accepting gifts from the Ward without prior court approval. Criminal charges could also result from misappropriation of funds, fraud, or theft.

Needless to say, litigation can surface quickly in these cases. To minimize liability, consult an attorney early in the appointment process. Communicate regularly with the attorney and be willing to address issues and conflicts as they arise.

Other Professionals Appointed to the Case

With the filing of a petition for appointment — Guardian or Conservator — the court appoints a court investigator to the case. With an allegedly incapacitated adult, the investigator interviews the protected person and files a written report. Examination by a doctor, psychologist, or registered nurse will be ordered with written reports also filed with the court. ARS §14-5303. The court appoints an attorney for the allegedly incapacitated adult, too. A Guardian ad Litem (GAL) may be appointed for the duration of the legal action as well.

9

What Is Probate Litigation?

Probate litigation stems from a dispute. An interested party objects or disagrees with some aspect of the case and seeks court intervention to resolve the issue. If validity of a Will is contested, for example, then probate litigation will be needed to establish the Will's authenticity.

Most informal cases are uncontested, moving through probate without litigation. Even if the estate is informally probated, arrange to have an attorney available to answer your questions.

What Probate Issues Require Litigation?

The matter litigated will depend upon how far along the case is in the probate process. With admission of the Will to probate, objections could come from a devisee, former spouse, a child, or creditor. If the challenge is successful, then the probate judge may admit an earlier Will, or not admit any Will and proceed under the laws of intestate succession. During administration of the estate, the surviving spouse may object to the Personal Representative's interpretation of the Will, among other things.

These are the types of challenges we often see in our probate litigation practice:

- **Will Invalidity.** This is a Will contest over the instrument's authenticity. Is this the decedent's most recent Will or codicil (amendment)?
- **Testamentary Capacity.** In drafting or executing the Will, there was undue influence over the testator or financial exploitation, fraud, duress, forgery, lack of testamentary capacity, or no witnesses to the signing. Did someone in a close relationship with the testator manipulate him or her for personal gain?
- **Will Interpretation.** Disputes arise over interpretation of Will provisions that conflict or

are ambiguous. Should the court examine the Will to provide clarification and instruction?

- **Objection to Appointment.** Objections arise over appointment of a Personal Representative, Trustee, Guardian, or Conservator. Does the surviving spouse object to the adult daughter's appointment as Personal Representative?

- **New Evidence.** Important testamentary instruments are discovered while the case is ongoing. Was a codicil, more recent Will, or revocation of trust found and is now being offered into evidence?

- **Family Disagreement.** Inability to reach family agreements or resolve disputes through settlement conferences lead to hearings, determinations, and orders. Are adult children of the deceased parent arguing over who should get what?

- **Creditor Disputes.** A creditor may object to actions by the Personal Representative that impact a claim. Was the landlord's rent claim rejected?

- **Estate Administration.** Devisees, beneficiaries, and heirs can challenge the Personal Representative's administration. Allegations of breach of fiduciary duty, conflicts of interest, unreasonable fees for services rendered, self-dealing, misappropriated funds, fraud, deliberate omissions, and more are possible. Did the Personal Representative treat the devisee unfairly in the distribution?

Probate litigation is not limited to Wills and intestate issues, of course.

What if there is a trust? There are many different types of trusts. Testamentary trusts. Living trusts. Special needs trusts. Revocable trusts and irrevocable trusts. Judicially imposed constructive trusts. The Superior Court has probate jurisdiction over matters of trust administration, too.

What if a testamentary trust did not name a specific person to serve as trustee? Or the person nominated rejects appointment? A valid trust will not fail for lack of a trustee, meaning the court will appoint someone to serve as the Trustee.

Other Probate Litigation Matters

Consider some other situations that require judicial intervention:

- **Trusts.** Problems with trust interpretation, trustee appointment, trust administration, trust modification, and property distribution are possible. Does a beneficiary object to the amount of income being distributed?

- **Constructive Trusts.** A constructive trust is created by the court and is an equitable remedy. Property belonging to the Conservatorship estate is being withheld. Can the court establish a constructive trust and require delivery of the property to the Conservator?
- **Powers of Attorney.** The agent exercised power of attorney after the principal's death, but before the agent received notice of the death. Can an asset be recovered by the estate if the agent transferred it after the principal's death?
- **Guardians or Conservators.** With minors and incapacitated adults, there are a number of challenges possible. Some are directed at appointment. Others are directed at how duties are carried out. Does the protected person object to appointment of the individual petitioning for Letters of Conservator?
- **Premarital Agreements.** These instruments often include provisions intended to be enforceable upon the death of a spouse, such as a plan for distribution of property. Terms in the prenuptial agreement may conflict with provisions in the Will. When the spouse died intestate, heirs may object to the postmarital agreement's planned division of investments or business interests. In these cases, the validity, enforceability, and interpretation of

the prenuptial agreement is likely to be challenged and vigorously litigated.

In probate practice, there may be a need for ancillary estate administration in Arizona with the main proceedings in another state. With probate in Washington State where the decedent resided, for example, ancillary administration in Maricopa County follows with a second home in Scottsdale. Ancillary administration is not unusual, but does open the door to another situation where litigation may be necessary.

10

Settlements, ADR, and Probate Appeals

As with all civil cases, settlement and alternative dispute resolution play an important role in helping people find solutions. Negotiation, mediation, and settlement conferences are an important part of the probate process. Whenever possible, parties are encouraged to reach family agreements and negotiated settlements.

The scope and duration of litigation depends upon the parties, the seriousness of the disputed matter, the size of the estate, the urgency of the situation, and other factors. In other words, probate litigation varies substantially from one case to the next.

We know protracted litigation has the potential to damage family relationships. Whereas cooperation, communication, and agreement can resolve many issues, if not all, and help keep families unified.

Try to be objective. Don't let emotional baggage over something that happened a long time ago interfere with the present.

Appealing a Final Judgment

Lastly, a party has the right to appeal the probate judge's final judgment or order. There is limited time within which to file Notice of Appeal — a party has only 30 days from the date of the final order.

Probate appeals must follow the court rules set forth in the *Rules of Civil Appellate Procedure*. Understand that the Court of Appeals does not retry the case, take testimony from witnesses, or examine new evidence. Instead, it reviews the official record from the probate court below and determines if the judge made an error of fact or law. Ordinarily, harmless errors will not change outcomes.

Sometimes cases are remanded (or sent back) to the probate court for further proceedings consistent with the appellate court's decision. This could be a probate hearing on admissibility of a newly discovered Will, for example. The appellate court can affirm or reverse the probate court's final judgment, wholly or partially. The Court of Appeals could order remand on one matter, affirm another, and reverse still another.

If a client is dissatisfied with the outcome of the case and desires review, then our probate attorneys will handle the appeal as well.

Scott David Stewart, Esq.

Born and raised in Phoenix, author Scott David Stewart is the founding attorney of Stewart Law Group. His vision was to establish a unique law firm singularly focused on the clients' experiences when dealing with difficult and often intensely emotional legal matters.

With eight office locations throughout the Valley of the Sun, today this influential law firm represents clients in all matters of divorce, child custody and family law, estate planning and probate, accident and personal injury, professional license defense, DUI defense, and general criminal defense.

Early in his professional career, Stewart was Deputy County Attorney in the Major Crimes Division of the Maricopa County Attorney's Office. As a felony prosecutor, he honed his trial skills and developed the strategies for success that he continues to implement today in all aspects of his law practice. Since its formation, Stewart Law Group has earned the trust and respect of clients from all walks of life.

Stewart is a member of the State Bar of Arizona, Maricopa County Bar Association, and American Bar Association. He has an AV Preeminent® attorney-rating from Martindale-Hubbell® and is also rated "Superb" by Avvo, Inc. Stewart Law Group is an accredited Arizona business with the Better Business Bureau having received an A+ rating.

With more than seven decades of combined legal experience, Scott Stewart and Stewart Law Group take on the most complex and challenging cases. To read more about the author, his recognitions, awards, and client testimonials, visit www.ArizonaLawGroup.com.

Brian G. Winter, Esq.

Brian G. Winter is an associate attorney with Stewart Law Group and has been a practicing attorney for 20+ years. A respected trial lawyer, Winter's practice includes estate planning, probate litigation, divorce and family law. He has a strong background in ADR (Alternative Dispute Resolution) and a special interest in mediation and collaborative divorce.

Born and raised in Fairfield, Connecticut, Winter obtained his BA in Government and Politics (1990) and his JD (1993) from St. John's University in Jamaica, Queens. In Connecticut where he later practiced, Winter in probate court served as a guardian ad litem and attorney for proposed Wards in conservator and guardianship proceedings and children in guardianship proceedings. Winter also served as a guardian ad litem and as counsel for children in family law matters, as well as serving as a family law Special Master to the court.

An experienced negotiator and litigator, Avvo, Inc., rated Winter "Pro" and "Superb" with a perfect 10-of-10 score. In addition, Winter has received the following awards and distinctions:

• *10 Best Attorney* •
American Institute of Family Law Attorneys – 2020

• *Top 10 Estate Planning Attorneys* •
Attorney and Practice Magazine – 2019

• *10 Best Attorney* •
American Institute of Family Law Attorneys – 2019

• *10 Best Estate Planning Attorney* •
American Institute of Legal Counsel – 2018

• *Lawyers of Distinction – 2017* •

• *10 Best Estate Planning Attorney* •
American Institute of Legal Counsel – 2017

• *Top Ten Ranking* •
National Academy of Family Law Attorneys – 2016

• *10 Best Family Law Attorneys* •
American Institute of Family Law Attorneys – 2016

• *10 Best Estate Planning Attorney* •
American Institute of Legal Counsel – 2016

Brian Winter is admitted to practice law in Arizona, Connecticut, Florida, and New York. He is also admitted to practice in the USDC for the District of Connecticut. Winter is a member of the State Bar of Arizona, Scottsdale Bar Association, and Maricopa County Bar Association where he served on the 2016 Board of Directors. Winter also serves on the Board of the Maricopa County Bar Association Family Law Section (2019 to present).

Made in the USA
Monee, IL
13 September 2026

62981946R00039